Moon Pussy 2019

A collection of flyers and pictures from 2019

©2019

HXCMIDI

THE ASS

PLASMA CANVAS

MOON PUSSY

ERASERHEAD AND THE FUCKERS

@ NUDE CITY RELIEF CENTER

8:30PM BE THERE OR GO TO JAIL

1.25.19

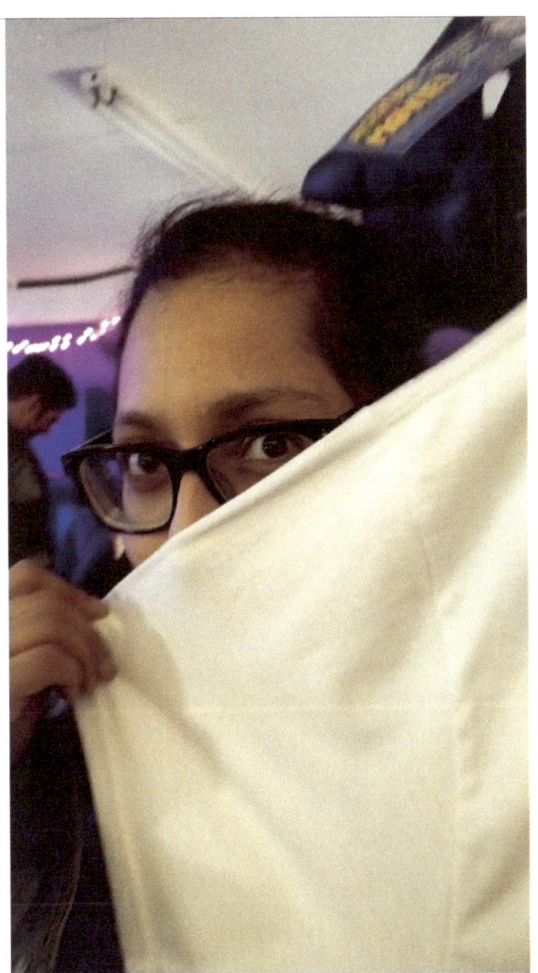

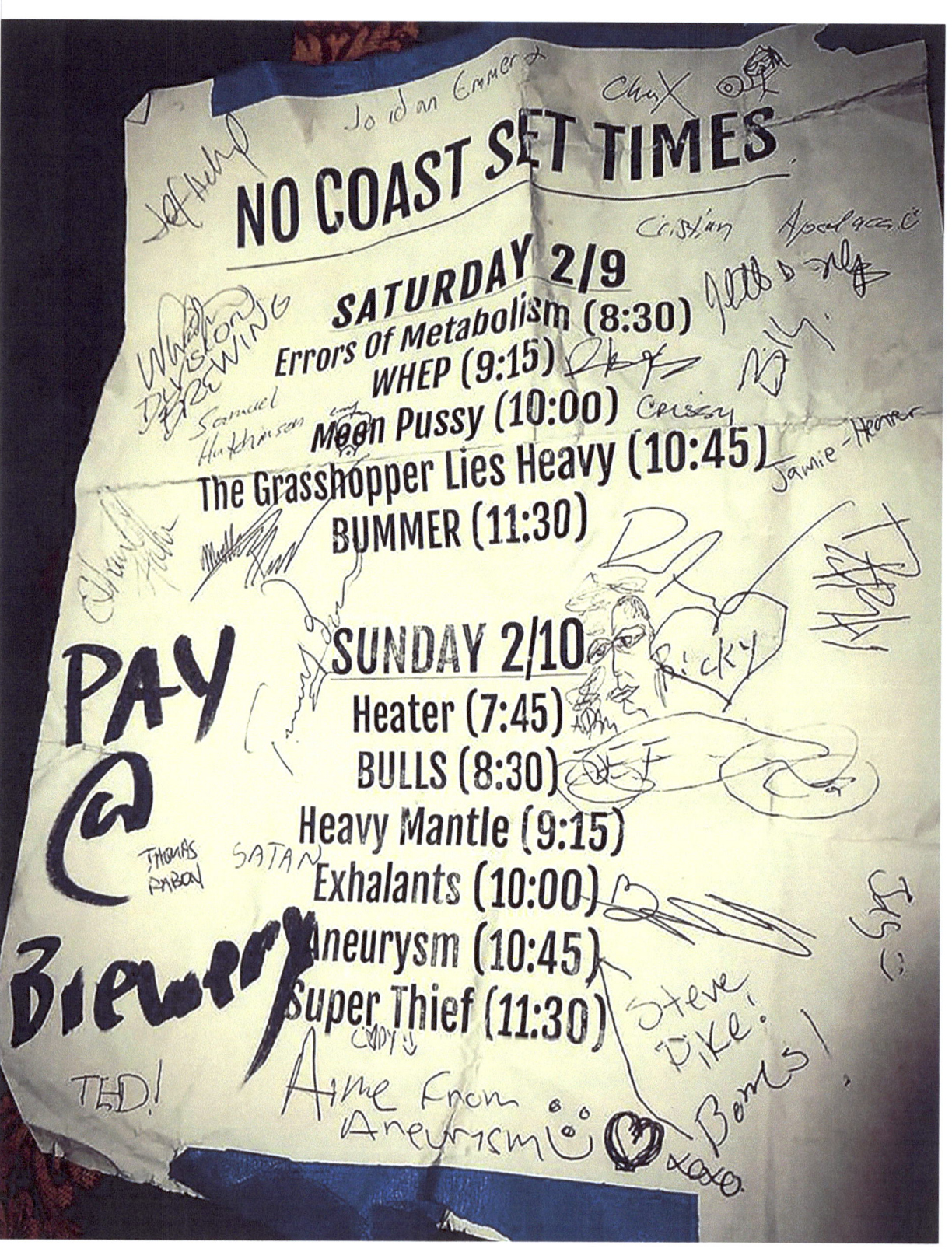

Rat Bites
Grave Moss
Moon Pussy
Dead Characters

BarBar
Feb 23rd

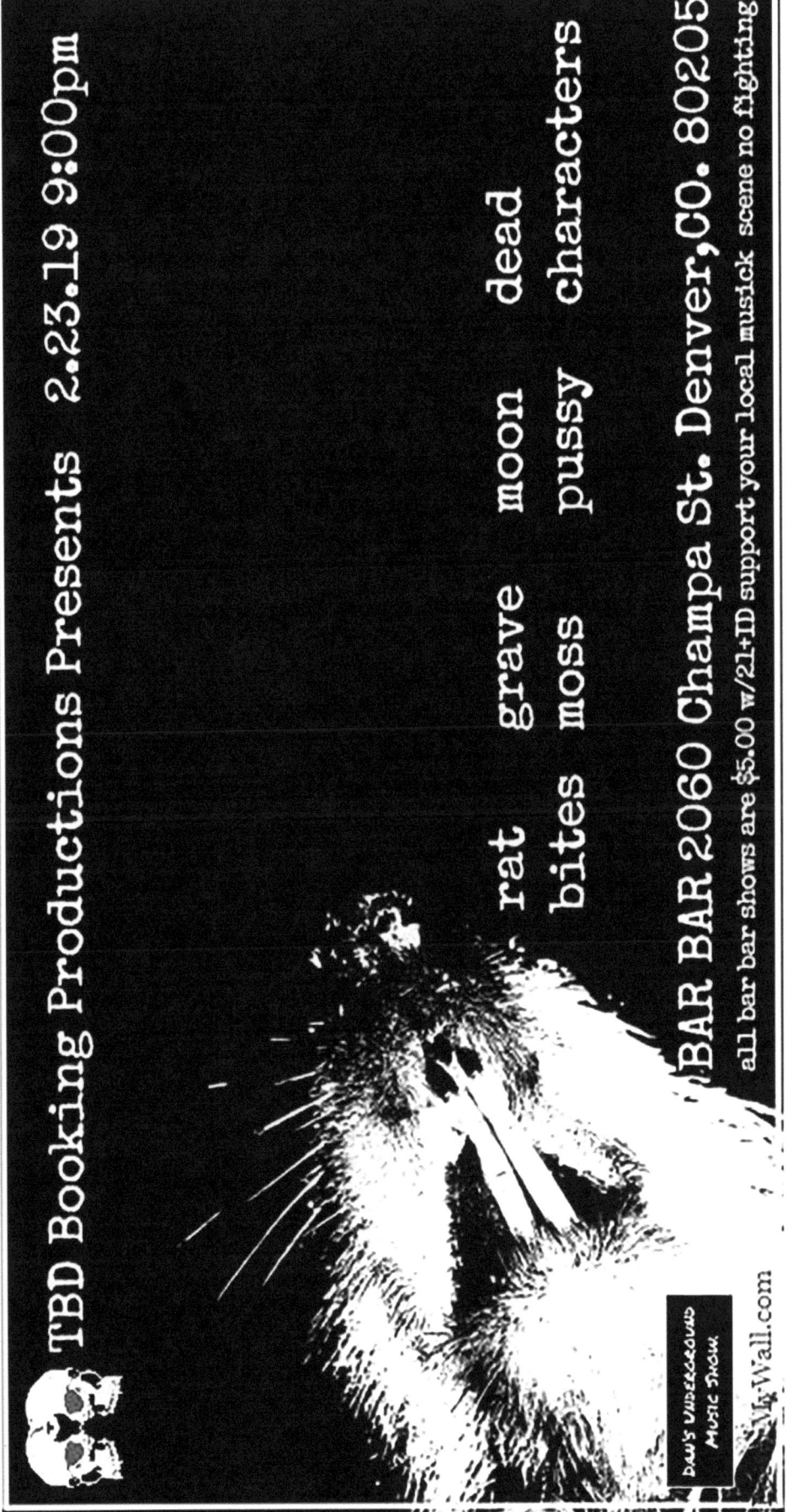

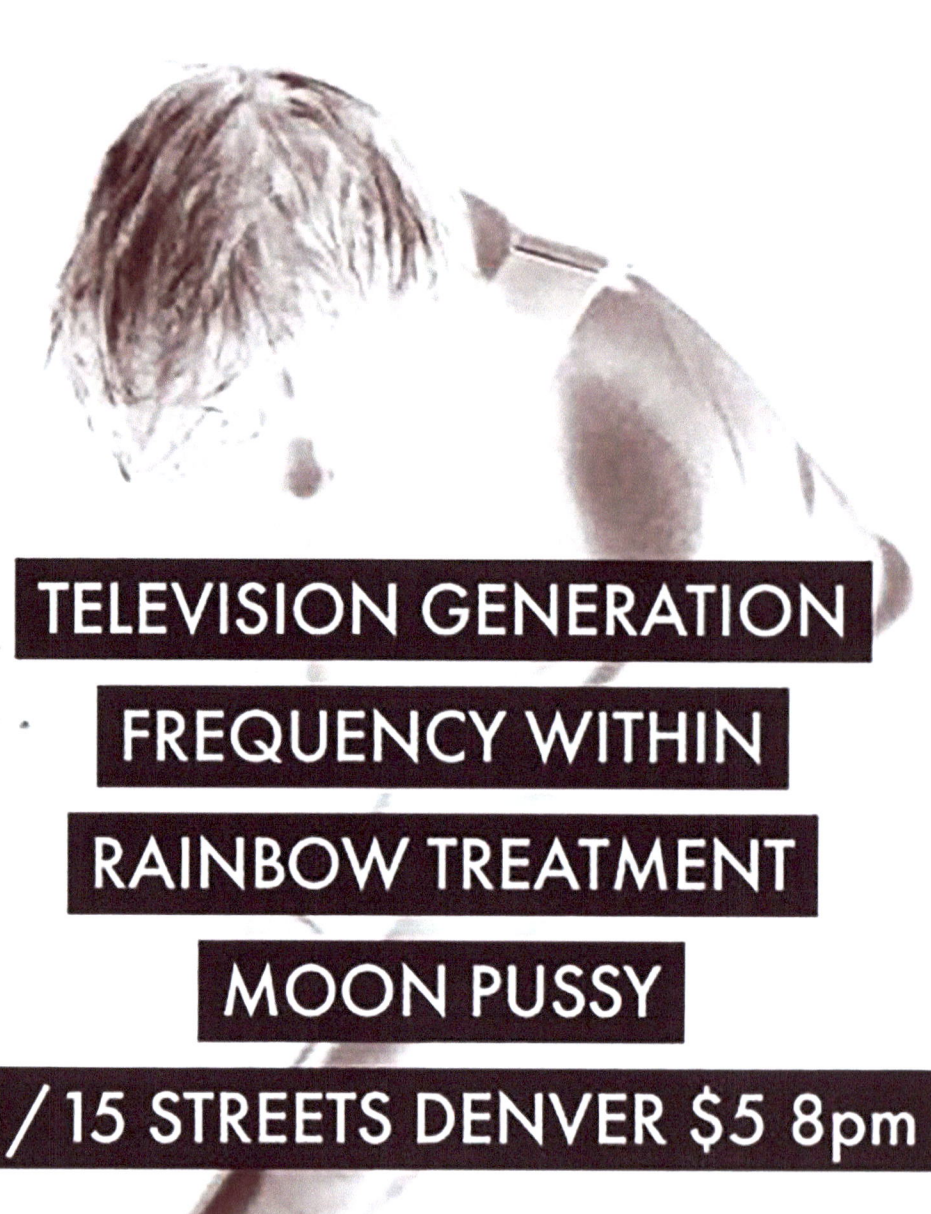

3.27.19
Wild Powwers,
Moon Pussy,
Shiny Around The Edges
@ Mutiny Information Cafe

PRF DENVER
APRIL 26-28, 2019

 A WEEKEND OF BEER, BBQ, & MUSIC

FRIDAY, APRIL 26
@ BLACK SKY 8:00 pm
DEAD CHARACTERS
NEW STANDARDS MEN
MODERN GOON
CLUTCH PLAGUE

BEER & BBQ PROVIDED!!!

SATURDAY, APRIL 27
@ THE BAKERY 2:00pm
SIMULATORS
THE OXFORD COMA (AZ)
MOON PUSSY
LAURIUM
CONAN NEUTRON AND
THE SECRET FRIENDS (WI)
HOOPER
SEWINGNEEDLE (IL)
FUTURE SCARS (NM)

SUNDAY, APRIL 28
@ THE BAKERY 2:00pm
FLOWLINES
50 MILES OF ELBOW ROOM
LITTLE BEARDS (TX)
FALSETTO BOY
CHURCH VAN
TEACUP GORILLA
PURPLE HONEY (SD)
THE GARY (TX)

 MORE INFO: http://tinyurl.com/PRFBBQDENVER

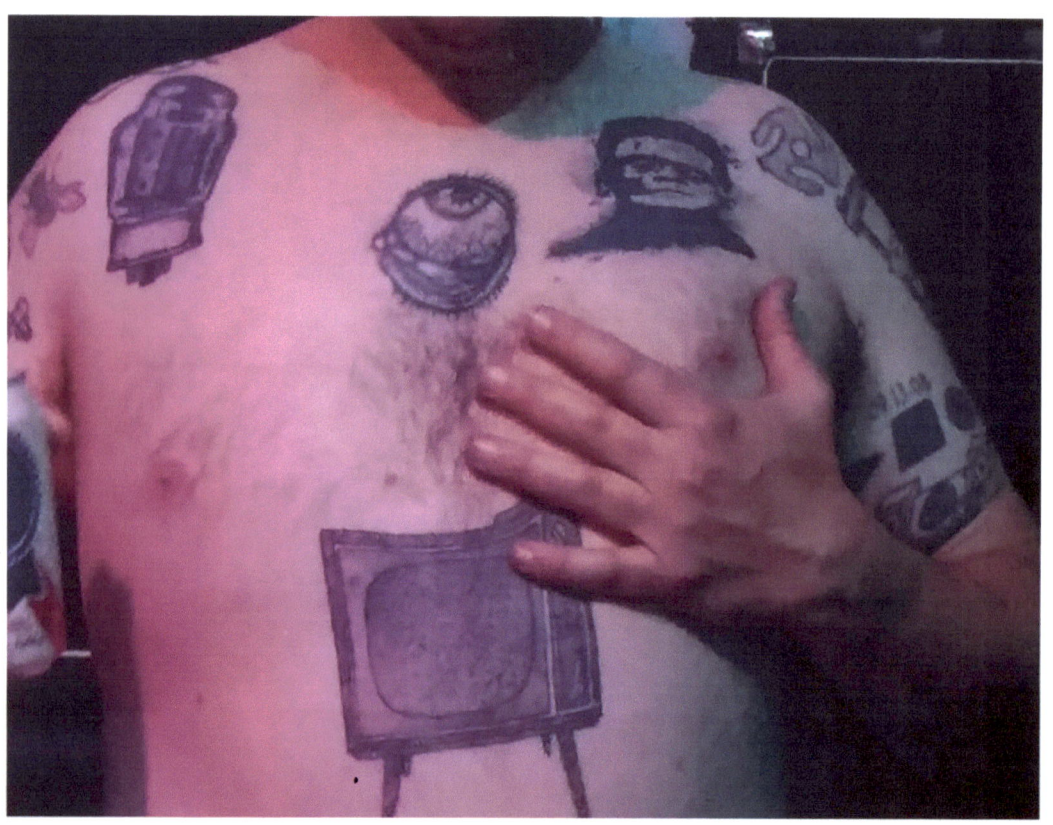

GHOST PUNK ROCK POTLUCK!

FIBBER
MOON PUSSY (Denver, CO)
cattleguard
FUTURE SCARS
NEW STANDARDS MEN (Denver, CO)
Clementine was Right
HOLY GARDEN DISTRICT

SAT. 6/8

GHOST   2889 TRADES WEST RD
4PM $5 SUGGESTED DONATION
BRING A DISH OR A SNACK TO SHARE!

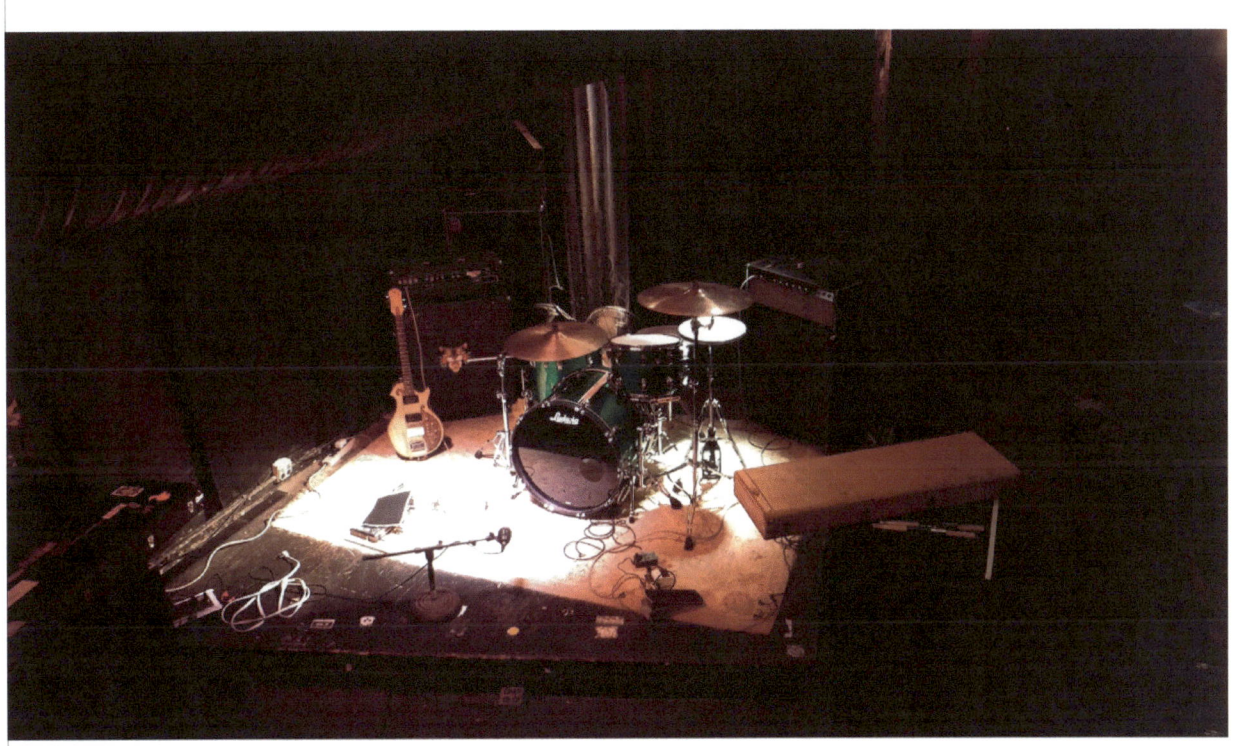

7/15 BROOKLYN @ ALPHAVILLE
W/ AVA MENDOZA, MOON PUSSY

HOARIES.BANDCAMP.COM

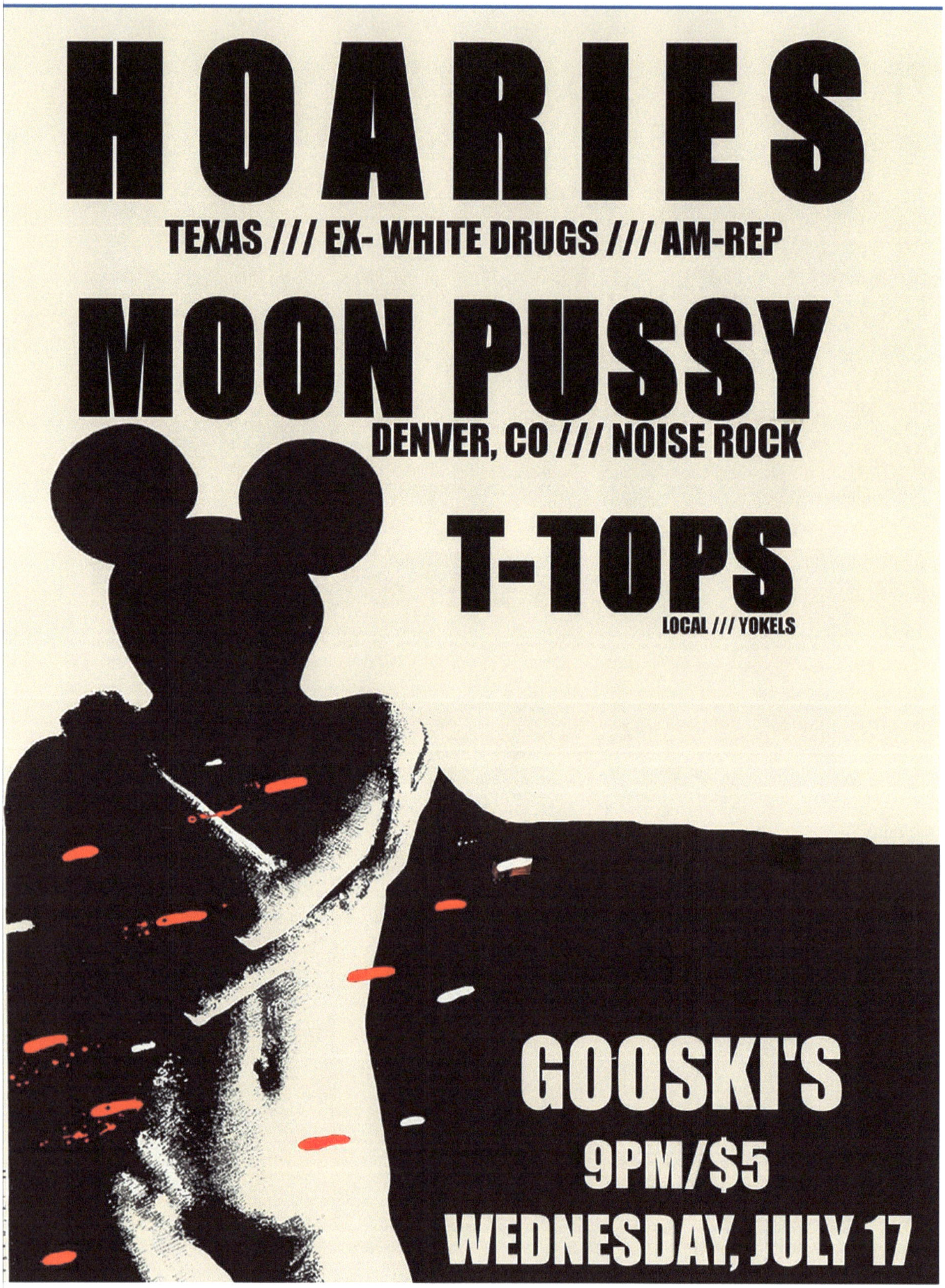

HOARIES
TEXAS /// EX- WHITE DRUGS /// AM-REP

MOON PUSSY
DENVER, CO /// NOISE ROCK

T-TOPS
LOCAL /// YOKELS

GOOSKI'S
9PM/$5
WEDNESDAY, JULY 17

July 18th Detroit

Hoaries, Moon Pussy, West Grand

The Yellow Rake #33 Zine Release and Simulators Record Release Party!

Music by:
SIMULATORS
Moon Pussy

↑ YOU'LL LIKE THESE BANDS

Readings by:
BRIAN POLK
KARL CHRISTIAN KRUMPHOLZ
CHARLY FASANO

← THESE FOLKS ARE ENTERTAINING

Friday, August 9th
All Ages
8 p.m.

BOOKS ○ RECORDS ○ COMICS ○ COFFEE
2 S. Broadway

RECORD COVER ↘

(NOT PICTURED: ZINE COVER)

MOON PUSSY

purple honey

New Standards Men

Warring Parties

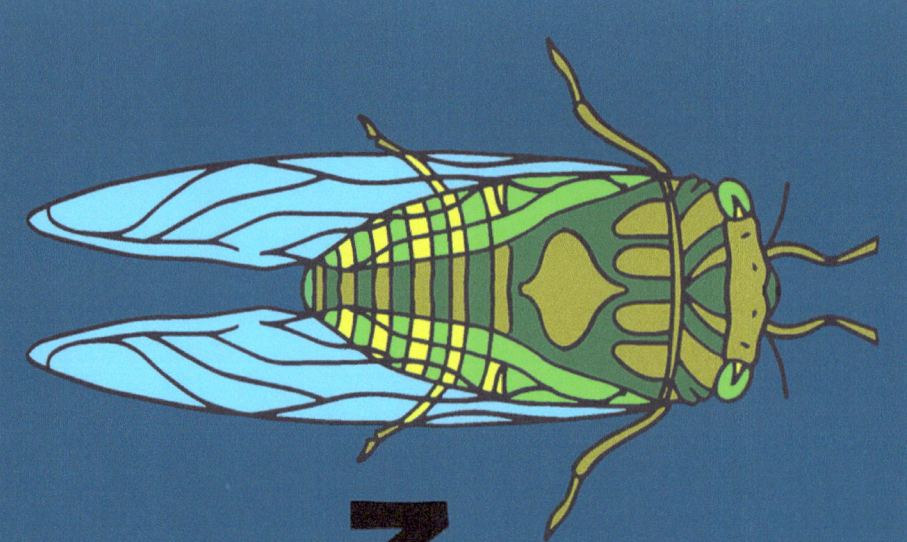

Prissy Whip
Moonpussy
New Standards Men

Oct 1st Rhinoceropolis

OCTOBER SATURDAY 12TH

GET SOME
CHERUBS

WITH SPECIAL GUESTS

MOON PUSSY

Moe's Original BAR B QUE

3295 S BROADWAY
ENGLEWOOD, CO
TICKETS @ WWW.MOESDENVER.COM

DOORS @ 8:00 PM
SHOW @ 9:00 PM
ALL AGES

Moon Pussy is:
Cory Hager - Drums
Cristina Cuellar - Bass / Vocals
Ethan A Hahn - Guitar

www.ingramcontent.com/pod-product-compliance
Lightning Source LLC
Chambersburg PA
CBHW041523220426
43669CB00002B/32